Thank you Mum

# Thank you Mum

## A *Heartwarmers*™ Gift Book

# Thank you Mum

A Heartwarmers™ Gift Book

©WPL 2002

Text by Anne Dodds

Illustration by Michael Hodgkinson

Printed in China

Published by WPL 2002

ISBN 1-904264-01-8

For information on other Heartwarmers™ gift books, gifts and greetings cards, please contact

WPL

14 Victoria Ind. Est. Wales Farm Road

London W3 6UU UK

Tel: +44 (0) 208 993 7268 Fax: +44 (0) 208 993 8041

email: wpl@atlas.co.uk

Mum,
this little book
is for you
as I wanted to say,
all the things
that go unsaid
as life goes on
each day.

You are just so special
and I really hope you know
you'll always mean
the world to me
wherever I may go.

I know that often I forget
to say these words to you,
but I wanted to say, Mum,
just how much I love you.

I really want to thank you
for all the wonderful things you do,
and I'd like to say, above all else,
Mum, thanks for being you.

Thank you Mum for being there
each day my whole life through,
to guide and reassure me
in everything I do.

Thank you Mum for being my friend
when no-one else was there,
for listening to my problems
and for showing that you care.

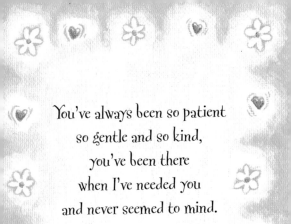

You've always been so patient
so gentle and so kind,
you've been there
when I've needed you
and never seemed to mind.

Thanks for standing up for me
and for making sure I know,
that no matter how my life turns out
you'll always love me so.

I hope you know beyond all doubt
how very much I care,
and how grateful I have always felt
just knowing you are there.

Of all the people in my life
you've always been the one,
who's shown an extra-special interest
in the things that I have done.

When I was a little child
it was you who dried my tears.
You always knew the magic words
that chased away my fears.

When I awoke each morning
the first thing I would see,
would be your happy, smiling face
gazing down at me.

It was you who gave me confidence
for each new step along the way,
reassuring me and guiding me
each and every day.

You've been there to congratulate
and to commiserate as well,
you were the one who picked me up
every time I fell.

I've always known
that you were proud
of my achievements
big and small,
but knowing
I was happy was
what you wanted
most of all.

You made my childhood special
in so many different ways,
and the memories will stay with me
forever come what may.

Every step of the way Mum
you have guided me through life.
You've listened and you've understood
and you've given the best advice.

I know that as I take my place
on life's long bumpy road,
you'll always be the one I turn to
to help me with my load.

It's true that sometimes you and me
haven't seen eye to eye,
but I know you want the best for me
you only want to try...

...to shield me from life's pitfalls,
which could leave me feeling sad,
by letting me have some benefit
from the experiences you've had.

Although I know you meant well
I still did things my own way,
and regretted not listening
to what you had to say.

Because of you, Mum,
I have learned
so many different things,
and now I know
I'm better prepared
for whatever life may bring.

Through all the ups and downs of life
you've always helped me see
that if I can keep on trying,
I'll be the best that I can be.

The values you have taught me
will always see me through.
They have shaped my character -
who I am and what I do.

Now I have the confidence,
not to be afraid,
but to bravely go ahead
with decisions I have made.

Sometimes things don't go as planned
and I make mistakes, it's true,
but I know before long
we'll laugh about it
together, me and you.

I think the most
important thing
that I have learned
from you,
is to be happy
with the way I am
and to be proud of what I do.

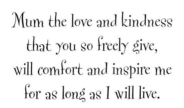

Mum the love and kindness
that you so freely give,
will comfort and inspire me
for as long as I will live.

Your wit and loving wisdom
are gifts I'll always treasure,
and the pride I feel when I'm with you
is much too great to measure.

If there's one thing
I am sure of
as life goes on each day,
it's that you mean
much more to me
than any words can say.

I'm sure you know
without a doubt
even if we are apart,
we'll always hold
a special place
within each
other's heart.

I hope you know that come what may
I'll always be there for you too,
and I wish you luck and happiness
in everything you do.

So for the person I am today
and for the one I will become,
thanks for everything you've done for me.
Thanks for being my Mum.

# A *Heartwarmers*™
## Gift Book

WPL

# Also available from Heartwarmers™

For a Special Friend

For my Sister

For You Mum

100 Reasons why I Love You

For my Husband

To a Good Friend

Believe in Yourself

For my Nan

I Love You Because...

For a Special Daughter

For a Special Mum